Alan Moore Spells It Out
On Comics, Creativity, Magic and much, much more

an interview by
Bill Baker

a Bill Baker Presents... book

PUBLISHING LLC.

Airwave Publishing, LLC
www.AirwavePublishing.com

Alan Moore Spells it Out On Comics, Creativity, Magic and much, much more

Airwave Publishing, LLC
airwavepublishing@yahoo.com
www.AirwavePublishing.com

isbn# 0-9724805-7-9

PRINTED IN CHINA by Regent Publishing Services Limited. Contact RegentNY2@aol.com for additional information.

First Printing 2005

Lost Girls©2005 Alan Moore and Melinda Gebbie

About the Bill Baker Presents ... series of books

Alan Moore Spells It Out is the first volume of the Bill Baker Presents ...series of books featuring in-depth interviews with the best and brightest, the pioneers and forefathers of the comic book medium, and other Pop Culture entertainments.

Bill Baker would like to take a moment to thank:

Alan Moore for his generosity of spirit and time, as well as his abiding patience and support throughout the long process of seeing this conversation into print.

Rich Maurizio for publishing this and the other Bill Baker Presents ... books. And for putting up with this particular brand of lunacy ... For years, no less.

Joel Meadows for his elegant design work, and particularly his unflagging friendship, support and assistance. Again, for years. First round's on me, mate!

José Villarrubia for the use of his wonderful photo on this book's cover, along with his unwavering and vocal support of my efforts.

Chris Staros, Brett Warnock and **Top Shelf** for permission to use the cover image, as well as their ongoing friendship and support. Guess the second round's on me, too.

A veritable host of other people, literally too many to name here, including the creators, publishers and support personnel, the fans, my fellow journalists and all the other good folks I've met and spoken with over the years, whether on or off the record, each of whom has helped me in ways large and small.

And, finally, **You**, The Reader, for picking up this book, opening the pages and making it all real again. Even if it's only for a second...

...Without each of you, none of this would have been possible, nor mean as much.

Illustration Credits

1 page 3 Alan Moore, et. al, ABC Sketchbook (© America's Best Comics, LLC) cover detail, #2 Alan Moore and Melinda Gebbie, Lost Girls (© Alan Moore and Melinda Gebbie), detail from the first cover for the abortive Kitchen Sink run, circa 1995, #3 Alan Moore and David Lloyd, et. al., V for Vendetta (© DC Comics), detail of Lloyd's character design for the titular character, first showcased in Warrior Magazine # 17.

4 page 8 Alan Moore, J. H. Williams III, Mick Gray, et. al., Promethea # 12 (© America's Best Comics, LLC.), detail of the Tarot "Art" card from page 16, found in volume 3 of the trade collections.

5 page 14 Alan Moore, Maxwell the Magic Cat (© 1979, 2005 Alan Moore), cover to volume 1 of the Acme/Eclipse trade collections. Long out-of-print.

#6 page 21 Alan Moore and Alan Davis, D.R & Quinch ©2001 Rebellion. Sketch from Titan collection.

#7 page 25 Alan Moore, David Lloyd, et. al., V for Vendetta (© 2005 DC Comics.), cover for the original 1990 American edition.

#8 page 32 Alan Moore and Eddie Campbell, Snakes and Ladders (©2001 Alan Moore and Eddie Campbell Comics), detail of the Tarot "Art" card.

9 page 36 Alan Moore and Eddie Campbell, From Hell (© 2001 Alan Moore and Eddie Campbell), detail of the frontispiece from the 1999 Graphitti Designs limited edition.

10 page 41 Alan Moore and Eddie Campbell, The Birth Caul (©1999 Alan Moore and Eddie Campbell Comics).

11 page 45 Alan Moore, Bill Sienkiewicz, et. al., Brought to Light (© 1989 Alan Moore and Bill Sienkiewicz, et. al.), cover.

12 page 49 Alan Moore, et. al., Violator (© Todd McFarlane Productions, Inc.), details of Moore's thumbnail sketches showcased in the back of the first issue.

13 page 54 Alan Moore, J. H. Williams III, Mick Gray, et. al., Promethea (© America's Best Comics, LLC.), the corrected "Mobius Strip" pages from the third trade collection.

14 page 59 Alan Moore, Dave Gibbons, et. al., Watchmen (© DC Comics, Inc.), details of rough layouts by Dave Gibbons from the 1987 Graphitti Designs limited edition.

15 page 63 Alan Moore, Dave Gibbons, et. al., Watchmen (© DC Comics, Inc.), detail from the second page of issue 3.

16 page 70 Alan Moore and David Lloyd, et. al., V for Vendetta (© DC Comics, music © V Songs), detail of the opening page from Book Two.

17 page 73 Alan Moore and Kevin O'Neill, The League of Extraordinary Gentlemen Volume 2, The Almanac
(™ & © 2003 Alan Moore & Kevin O'Neill)

 #18 page 74 Alan Moore and Eddie Campbell, Snakes and Ladders (©2001 Alan Moore and Eddie Campbell Comics), panel detail.

19 page 75 Alan Moore and Kevin O'Neil, et. al., The League of Extraordinary Gentlemen, The Absolute Edition, vol. 2 (™ & ©2003 Alan Moore & Kevin O'Neill), detail of the script book title page drawing of Moore by O'Neill.

INTRODUCTION

H ello, Bill Baker, freelance journalist and writer, here. For the past eight years I've worked full time covering the comic book industry. And while I've written any number of articles, reviews, and variously-themed columns for print and online publications, I've perhaps become best known for my in-depth, often career-spanning, interviews.

The job's perfect for me, really, since I'm fascinated by the creative process and how it manifests itself differently in each individual, although I'm unable to fully articulate the origin of my interest. Perhaps it's because the journey of the artist reflects – and is, in turn, reflected by – their work in large and small ways, and thus reveals truths about them and, by extension, all of us that might not otherwise be apparent. Maybe it's because, as a writer, I'm always looking to improve my craft, to discover that pitch-perfect tone that is my voice alone. Or it just could be due to the fact that I once mined similar territory in a seemingly unrelated field as an actor, director, designer and producer while working on my advance degrees and as an assistant professor of theatre. But, really, it's more likely because, at heart, I'm truly interested in how others create, what they go through to make their dreams real, and the means they employ in refashioning their fantasies into imaginary worlds filled with characters who live and breath, love and hate, live and die ... even if it's "just" on paper, even if it's "only" for the fleeting instant it exists in some unnamed reader's thoughts.

Admittedly, mine is a pursuit of one of the more ephemeral and subjective of human experiences. If, as Steve Martin noted, "Writing about Art is like Dancing about Architecture," imagine the Herculean task facing those who wish to speak extemporaneously on the subject, no matter how articulate they typically might be. It's often difficult at best for even the most fluent of folks to convey coherently their memories and impressions of their revelatory moments of creation, much less communicate the deeper, multilayered meanings of that experience and how those forces have affected the resulting art. However, I've happily discovered that, given the opportunity and proper venue, most comic book creators prove to be quite eloquent when given the chance to discuss the long, often hard road that they trod while carrying their projects to completion. To say that their eagerness and enthusiasm to share their gifts, along with their obvious conversational skills, have aided the work of this particular journalistic journeyman is an understatement of criminal proportions. Quite simply, I am indebted to each of the good people I've talked with during my career, and am deeply thankful for their acts of kindness, small and larger, as well as their generosity of spirit and time.

However, that willingness to share has to be balanced with an acceptance that deadlines often preclude the kinds of longer conversations that me and many creators prefer to have. Often, getting forty five minutes to an hour to talk on record with someone who is on a monthly, or even bimonthly, book schedule can be difficult, so it's easy to imagine the scheduling nightmares faced by those creators who are working on multiple monthly titles, no matter how willing they might be to talk.

Which makes the following interview with Alan Moore all the more unique and interesting. When I called Alan on the 16th of September, 2002, I hoped that he might be able to spare forty five minutes, or perhaps an hour, to talk about his working methods.

Imagine my surprise and gratitude when we said goodbye nearly five hours later, having recorded over three hours of incredibly insightful and ultimately practical advice and commentary from Alan on how he honed his craft throughout his life and career. Of course, we also touched upon any number of other topics, both personal and professional, during the course of our conversation, but the focus always returned to the topic of making comics and other art.

I've always found books featuring Alan Moore's work to be entertaining, thought-provoking and inspiring. It's my hope that this book will offer you all that, and more..
Enjoy!

Bill Baker

from the BFD Studios
lost in the wilds of Northern Michigan, USA
Sept., 2005

Promethea ®., ™ & ©America's Best Comics, LLC

"I think that storytelling and creation are very close to the center of what magic is about"

All the Colours of Magic: Alan Moore on Creativity and Creating Comics

Bill Baker: Would it be fair to say that words in general, as well as storytelling and the act of creation, hold a special kind of magic for you?

Alan Moore: I think that storytelling and creation are very close to the center of what magic is about. I think not just for me, but for most of the cultures that have had a concept of magic, the manipulation of language, and words, and thus of stories and fictions, has been very close to the center of it all. I mean in some senses, all of humanity's gods, since Paleolithic times, are in some senses a fiction. That is not meant to disparage the entities in question, because I hold fiction in a very special regard. I think that some fictions almost have, well a life of their own in a very special sense. The actual word itself, language itself, to me seems to be the primal technology.

   I mean, when people talk about computers, or video games, or the latest sort of piece of hardware that's available, they'll talk about it as new technology. Those things are *fruits* of technology. Technology is actually *writings about* a body of knowledge, or technique; that's the "logy" part of the word, which comes from the Greek *logos*. Basically, it says to me that language is the *initial* technology upon which everything else is based. I think you could probably make a good argument, and many people have made it, that consciousness itself can't actually happen without language. That we need words – words such as I, me, myself – before we can have thoughts that are of any use to us. Yes, we have *awareness* before that point, we'll be aware of pain and pleasure, but we won't really have any way of talking about those sensations until we have words for them, until we have words for our self.

So it seems to me that *all* culture, not just magic, but all *culture* is probably predicated upon language. I don't think it's technology that we completely understand. I think that there are mysteries in language and consciousness which could preoccupy us for hundreds of years, but which we really pay very little attention to. There is the big mystery, of course, as to why we have stories at all.

It would seem that, pretty soon after man had come down from the trees, yes, he found some form of shelter, he found something to eat, he found the means of making a fire, or whatever; but amongst his very first priorities would seem to have been drawing a kind of primitive comic strip explaining how he found the place to stay, the things to eat, and all the rest of it. Now, nature is not known for frilly and purposeless decorations. Everything in the behavior of a species is generally geared towards that species' survival and progress. Since it would seem that art and storytelling have been amongst our very earliest urges, I can only assume that these fictions, these sort of lightweight, throwaway little fables that we've been generating for centuries, must have some importance in what it is that makes us human, and in the human story.

So, yeah, personally, the act of creation, I find it mysterious. You can probe into that mystery, you can investigate that mystery using tools of technique and things that you can learn. But at the center of writing, at least for me, there is a very profound mystery that you could probably *never* hope to penetrate simply by using logic, common sense, reason, or all of the tools that we usually approach everything else with.

There is something very magical at the heart of writing, and language, and storytelling. The gods of magic in the ancient cultures, such as Hermes and Thoth, are also the gods of writing. I think that you only have to look at most so-called magic to see how much it relies upon the manipulation of language. You have invocations and evocations if you're a magician; you also have those things if you're a poet. And they mean pretty much the same thing in both cases. In magic, you will have your grimoires, your big, dark book of magic secrets. *Grimoires* is simply a fancier French way of spelling "grammar". To cast a spell, as far as I understand it, is simply to spell. The terminology of magic, and the terminology of language are almost identical. I mean, Aleister Crowley called magic "a disease of language." Something that inevitably emerges from the basic structure of language. That, in a way, our consciousness is made of language. We can't help it. We can't really think of anything unless we have words for it.

George Orwell, in *1984*, with his "newspeak" idea, the idea that a tyrannical government might actually be able to *limit* the vocabulary and language of a population, and in doing so, because people no longer had so rich a language, no longer had so many *words* that they were capable of knowing, then they would not have so many *concepts* that were within their grasp. That you could limit the intelligence and consciousness of a population simply by limiting their language. It would seem to me that's probably true, and also that the converse is probably true. That if you expose people to a more interesting and more open form of language, then you might actually expand their consciousness into areas that they perhaps hadn't thought about or considered before.

So, *yeah*, I'd say that, to me, writing is the most magical act of all, and is probably at the heart of every magical act.

BB: Was this always true for you, or was there a moment when you had an epiphany and realized all of this?

AM: I've always been interested in writing ever since I could write, from primary school onwards. My favorite part of the lessons that I was being given was always composition – writing essays, making up stories. Yeah, I've always been a sort of compulsive fantasist. It wasn't until fairly recently, when I was about forty, eight or nine years ago, that I started to see these things in terms of magic. But it's always been a motivating force in my life. I wanted, from a very early age, to create characters and create stories about them. This would even go back to when I'd play as a child.

I was thinking about this the other day. I was looking at some of the toys that are available at the moment, where you can get, if you want, action figures of the entire Justice League of America, Justice Society of America, all of the Silver Age villains, all of these sort of great characters of yesteryear. And I was thinking that, at the time, when I was eight or nine years old and reading those comics, I would have *killed* for a set of action figures that actually reflected the characters in the comics that I was reading. But they weren't available then. If they had been available, I wouldn't have been able to afford them.

So what I had to do instead was to take the simple, ordinary toy soldiers that I happened to have lying around, and invest them with something. If I had a spare Indian chief character that was left over from some cowboy and Indian soldiers, then I would probably say that this was some sort of Indian medicine man with supernatural powers. Perhaps he'd traveled across time to be in this sort of superhero group that I was assembling from these tiny, nondescript plastic figures. If I had a toy soldier that was obviously from a different set of soldiers because he was six times as big as any of the other toys in the collection, then I'd try and turn this into a plus by saying that this was Gigantic Man, and so on. I'd have a ball of plasticine that previously had been ... Oh, perhaps you don't call it plasticine over there; it's Playdoh, or modeling clay, something like that. Well, it starts off as lots of different rainbow colors, but after you've had it for two days it's just a maroon-brown blob. That was my shape-shifting, amoeboid villain from another galaxy when I was eight.

My point is that perhaps these days, when any character that you've ever seen on television or read about in a comic book or seen in a movie, you can go out and buy any number of plastic toys that are concerned with that character, any amount of merchandise, a child these days is not really given any great impetus to create their *own* characters out of their own imagination. In some ways, I'm really, really glad that there weren't cheap, freely available Justice League of America toys when I was seven, because if there had been, I might never have become a comic book writer. I might never have found what fun was to be had in the exercise of the imagination. The imagination is like a muscle, and I think that in a lot of people that muscle tends to atrophy, so that they don't really use their imagination, they're not really encouraged to use their imagination, everything is served up for them prepackaged. They never have to create anything for themselves.

Whereas from my earliest years, my favorite plaything was my imagination. And I really do think that that was what propelled me along the course that lead me to the point where I am today. I think that it's always been there in my life, that urge towards creation, towards fantasy, towards using the imagination.

It's probably dictated what most of my reading material has been since I was four years old, since I first learned to read, and it's certainly dictated the kind of life that I've had, and the career that I've chosen. That's always been a factor. And like I say, I do worry about people these days who perhaps have their imaginations spoon-fed to the point where they end up with imaginations that are perhaps enfeebled in some way.

BB: Did you want to write comics when you were a kid?

AM: I didn't know to start with, that people actually <u>did</u> write comics. I think for a while I imagined that, I don't know, these things just emerged on the page somehow. I really wasn't thinking about the fact that people wrote and drew these things when I first started reading comics. I was just completely gripped by the adventures of the various brightly costumed heroes.

After a while, however, probably when I was getting on to the age of ten-eleven-twelve, around that mark, I did start to become aware that, yes, that there were real people who did apparently make their livings drawing and writing all these wonderful stories that I was reading every month. And I think at that point, I would never have dared imagine that I might one day work in comics. But, by the time when I had got around to daring to imagine that, I probably

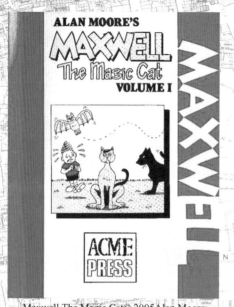

Maxwell The Magic Cat© 2005Alan Moore

"When I first got into comics, it was as a cartoonist, writing and drawing regular strips in a local newspaper"

would have imagined that I would have been an artist, rather than a writer. I did still have delusions of adequacy as an artist until my mid-twenties. I mean, when I first got into comics it was as a cartoonist, writing and drawing regular strips in a local newspaper over here, and in one of the national music papers. Which was a weekly gig, and which I'd hoped would improve my art to the level where I was no longer as embarrassed by it as I frankly was. This didn't turn out to be the case. After I'd been doing for a couple of years, I realized that I would never be able to draw well enough and/or quickly enough to actually make any kind of decent living as an artist. But I did realize that in having done a couple of years of a weekly comic strip that I had, almost incidentally, learned how to tell a serialized story. That my writing might actually be a better bet than my drawing.

Now, when I'd been a teenager, I'd done both. I contributed to local arts projects and magazines. I'd written poetry, probably because, like most teenagers, I was under the illusion that poetry was actually easy to write. I mean, *bad* poetry *is* easy to write. [General laughter] Good poetry, perhaps a lot trickier. But I'd be doing illustrations, and I'd be doing writing. I've always loved writing, so it seemed like an obvious shift of emphasis when I realized that my drawing abilities were limited, to say the least. I had still learned, over a couple of years of doing a weekly serialized strip, I had learned something about the mechanics of telling a story on demand every week that was at least interesting enough to keep the readers entertained, and to stop the editor from replacing it with something more commercial.

Since I'd been about eleven or twelve, I've probably nurtured a secret hope that one day I'd work in comics. I probably thought of that, at first at least, as being an artist. But when I got to my mid-twenties, and kind of wised up a little, I kind of realized that writing would be a lot quicker. I'd got a lot more control over how I wrote than how I drew. I could describe a person in words very quickly, while actually drawing them would be a lot trickier for me. So that was probably why I made the shift, and I'm very glad that I did. I don't think it was any great loss to the world of art, quite frankly, when I became a writer.

BB: How did you learn the craft, in general? Did some classes help you with that, or did you basically learn by doing it?

AM: Well, the thing that helped me to learn the craft, as I suspect is the case with everybody, with every writer, is reading. You have to enjoy stories as a reader before you're going to get that urge to think, "I wonder if I could do something like this?" or, "I bet I could do something better than this," or whatever urge it is that sort of makes us decide to actually pick up a pen and try it ourselves. I think that you read some books, and they would fill you with an awe and a realization of what it was to be a writer. You'd read things like Mervyn Peake's *Titus Groan* and *Titus Alone* and *Gormenghast*, where you start to get a sense of what a marvelous thing language is, and what it can do in the right hands.

  How, by just manipulating these twenty-six letters, people can conjure up characters so vividly that you'll read about them when you're fifteen, and you'll remember them for the rest of your life; when you've long forgotten real people that you made the acquaintance of, that you'll still remember these complete fictions that were just conjured up out of thin air by the author of whatever book it was that you happened to be so impressed by.

  I think it's when you have a love of stories as a reader, when you'll read something and you start to also read it with a critical eye, and an appreciation for a neatly pulled-off trick, or a beautiful drift of language. You start to see qualities in writing that you admire, that you would like to appropriate, and that probably leads – I'm only speaking for myself, here – but when I was a teenager, I'd write stuff that was obviously, and embarrassingly, a slavish, amateurish imitation of William Burroughs or whoever else I happened to be infatuated by at the time. And, for a while, I kind of felt as if I didn't have a style of my own at all, because I seemed to be just a mirror for whichever writer impressed me.

After a while, you tend to find that you absorb your influences and they become covert rather than overt. They become sort of intrinsic rather than explicit. They become part of you. And you start to realize that all of those great artists, those unique artists, that you worshipped, that of course they, in turn, were influenced by lots and lots of different things – different artists, different experiences – that somehow all got squashed together to end up as their unique style. And then you've taken something from them, something from somebody else, you've stirred them in together with your own life experiences, your own inclinations and tendencies, and what will come out in the end will uniquely be you, no matter how many influences you've absorbed. In fact, the more the better.

If you only ever allow yourself to be influenced by one person, then you'll probably end up as pretty much a pale shadow of that person, as an understudy. Much better to allow yourself to be influenced by a hundred people, a thousand people. That way it'll be a much tastier broth that is the pool that you're drawing your talent and your stories from.

BB: Who are some of the other people who had some kind of influence on you, along with Peake and Burroughs?

AM: Well, it's an immense list. I learned to read at the age of four or five. I remember my parents teaching me to read before I went to school, because there was a *dread* of illiteracy, because illiteracy was fairly prevalent in the area where I grew up. It was a working class area, and so, yeah, there were a lot of families where there was one or more members of the family that simply couldn't read. And I think, in my family at least, there was a kind of dread of that. That to be illiterate would be a terrible thing. So my mum and dad really made an issue of teaching me and my brother to read before we went to school. Which was excellent.

I joined a library by the time I was five. I gravitated towards stories about magic, whether they were the fairy stories that I must have been read from childhood, or the myths and legends that

I very soon fixated upon. As soon as I first joined the children's library, I was taking out all of these various children's versions of the classic myths: the Norse myths, the Arthurian legends, the Robin Hood story. And the main reason why I was fascinated with these was because they had this element of magic in them. You could read and experience things in these stories that you could not experience in real life. People in these stories could do anything. Anything could happen in a myth or legend. It was a different dimension to everyday life, and it was one that excited me and fascinated me. And so probably as I grew up I would tend to naturally gravitate towards things that had an element of the fantastic in them. Like I say, that was a lot of myths and legends.

At the age of seven, when I first discovered American comic books, these characters resembled the Greek gods or Norse gods of my other reading, and so they were a natural choice. I was reading lots and lots of science fiction from an early age. Lots of ghost and horror stories. People like M. R. James, H. Russell Wakefield, all of the classic English ghost stories. I'd be borrowing these huge anthologies from the library, and frighten myself.. Algernon Blackwood, people like that. I was probably far too young to appreciate all the nuances of the stories, but I knew what I liked.

And then, throughout my teenage years, I'd have passions and fads. Very early on I had a brief flirtation with Dennis Wheatley, which I think that, at least in this country, you have to kind of read Dennis Wheatley when you're eleven; much older than that, and it will be laughable rubbish. But if you're eleven, it can be quite a heady mixture of Satanism and the supernatural. I was reading Lovecraft very early on. In terms of science fiction, I remember Ray Bradbury being an early favorite when I discovered his work. I would read pretty omnivorously. When I started to read sword and sorcery, I became very, very fond of Michael Moorcock's material.

From the Moorcock connection, I gravitated to *New Worlds* when I was about fourteen or fifteen, which was the science fiction magazine that Moorcock was editing over here at the time, and which was *incredibly* revolutionary. Moorcock and his fellow contributors   people like J. G. Ballard, Barrington Bayley, M. John Harrison, John Sladek – had more or less written a new manifesto stating that science fiction should not deal with its usual escapist tropes, but instead should deal with the actual, real issues of the future. What would the psychologies of the future be like? What was society of the present day really like? What was going on in our heads? They were using science fiction as a ...I think a quote at the time stated that science fiction was the only literature that was fully capable of describing the present, which I thought sounded kind of good to me. And so through *New Worlds* I discovered authors who were a lot more hip, a lot more experimental, a lot more radical, and I started to enjoy them. It was *New Worlds* that led me to William Burroughs. Burroughs led me to the rest of the Beat writers. My literary tastes pretty much then exploded all over the place.

At the moment, my favorite writers who are currently producing stuff would include people like Ian Sinclair, Cormac McCarthy – an *excellent* American writer – and innumerable others. I'm very promiscuous and fickle. I'll have a new favorite every couple of days, if I'm lucky, and I'm always looking for new novelists to absorb. I've been quite impressed with Glenn Gold's *Carter Beats the Devil*, there's a thumping good yarn. And, of course, Michael Chabon, with *The Adventures of Cavalier and Clay*, very good book. Mark Danielewski with *House of Leaves*, excellent book, and *marvelous* structural stuff he's doing there, a wonderful piece of construction.

And that's just the American authors. There's some great young authors that are coming up over here; Laura Hird, who has written some blackly comic but touching social realist stuff. I enjoy obscure decadent authors like David Lindsay, who wrote *A Voyage to Arcturus*. At the moment I seem to be going through a fad of those kind of authors who wrote from around about 1900 to about 1940, a lot of them British. Jack Trevor Story has always been a favorite. Yeah, I'm pretty omnivorous. I could probably just ramble all night, sort of mentioning names.

But, like I say, the more people you're influenced by, the better it is. If you can take tiny little things from a thousand authors, that's much better than taking everything from one author.

BB: From what you said earlier, it sounds like you learned how to tell a sequential story by doing those strips for a few years.

AM: Uh-huh.

BB: The reason I ask is because there's an apocryphal tale I've heard more than once, which holds that Steve Moore actually sat down with you and explained some of the basic grammar of comic storytelling at some point early in your career.

AM: That's not entirely apocryphal. It's pretty much what happened.

What it was was that, when I decided that I wanted to try writing for comics rather than being a cartoonist, because I've known Steve Moore since I was fourteen, and Steve had been writing in comics since he was a teenager, he was the obvious person to ask. So I went to him and said, "Look, how do you actually lay out a script?" and Steve showed me how to lay out a script. So I went away and I wrote I think it was a Judge Dredd script, because I got the idea that I could just propose this to *2000AD*, and if they liked it, they'd accept it and then everything would be dandy. When I'd done the script I gave it to Steve, and Steve went through it brutally with a red pen and sort of said everything that I needed to know. He was saying things like, "This panel description is unclear. You've given the artist two moments to choose from in this one picture. Tidy that up." "This balloon is too long. There are far too many words in this panel." "Why is this caption necessary when, if the artist is doing his job properly, the reader should be able to see everything that is happening, so it doesn't really need a caption to underline it." All of these things. And they all made perfect sense.

I went through, rewrote the story taking Steve's suggestions into

D.R & Quinch©2005 Rebellion

"In a short story, you've maybe got four or five pages in which you have to create all of the characters, the whole world in which they exist"

account, and then sent it in to Alan Grant at *2000 AD*, who was one of the best editors that *2000AD* ever had. And Alan wrote back saying why they couldn't use it, because basically they've got a perfectly excellent writer for Judge Dredd already in John Wagner, and that they certainly didn't need anybody else, which made sense to me. But Alan said that he thought that my storytelling style showed promise, and asked would I like to try my hand at a couple of the "Future Shock" short stories that they were running at the time? So I did.

My first couple were turned down, but Alan would write letters explaining why they were turned down. Eventually, he wrote a letter saying, "Look, if you just changed this, this, and this, I think this one might be acceptable." So I made the changes according to what he'd suggested, he accepted it, and it was my first sale to *2000AD.*

Around this time, I'd started also selling work to *Dr. Who Weekly*. They were little back-up strips, featuring minor Dr. Who villains, and characters, and monsters that British Marvel sometimes needed. So this was great. At the time, I really, really wanted a regular strip. I didn't want to do short stories. I wanted to do regular, ongoing series that would bring in regular money. <u>But</u>, that wasn't what I was being offered. I was being offered short four or five page stories where everything had to be done in those five pages. And, looking back, it was the best possible education that I could have had in how to construct a story.

In a short story, you've maybe got four or five pages in which you have to create all of the characters, the whole world in which they exist. You have to set up the story, you have to bring it to a satisfying resolution. In fact, you have to do everything that you would normally do in a novel, but on a much smaller scale, and you have to do it in five pages. And that is tricky, but if you do enough short stories, you will eventually learn everything that you need in terms of basic craft that you can later <u>expand</u> to fill any size of narrative that you want. The same basic structure that you'd bring to a short five page story, it's still going to have a beginning, middle and an end. If you're doing a twenty-four page story, or a twelve issue series, or a massive graphic novel, then it will still have to have a beginning, a middle and an end. And if you've done a whole bunch of short stories, where you've tackled those very problems time and time and time again – "How do I start this story with a bang?" "What would be the most perfect ending for this story?" – by the time you graduate to something longer than five pages, you have all the ammunition and the abilities you need to write anything you want. To write huge, massive epics. Because you will have a sense of all the elements. You will have a sense of it, perhaps on a smaller scale, but you'll know what everything is, what it does, where it fits. You can just scale up the work accordingly if you start out with four page stories, yet you'll find yourself wishing that you could maybe have a twelve page story because just think what you could do with all those extra pages! You'd be able to give depth to the characters that you perhaps couldn't give them in a four page story. You'd be able to develop subplots, or things like that.

Consequently, when I was first offered a twenty-four page story on my first issue of *Swamp Thing*, I was delirious. But I wasn't lost, I wasn't floundering. I realized that the same rules that applied to the four and five page stories would apply just as readily to an individual issue of *Swamp thing*, or to my *run* on *Swamp Thing*, which turned out to be forty-five issues or something. My run on *Swamp Thing*, each issue has its own internal structure, and there is an overall structure to the development of the narrative and of the character. You learn that structure on the small scale with throwaway short stories, and if you learn it well enough, you will then be able to apply it to *absolutely* anything. It's the same set of skills that Tolstoy applied to *War and Peace*, or that any writer ever applied to any work of whatever size.

BB: It sounds like that concept of structure has informed everything you've done.

AM: Yeah. Because if you've got a good enough basic grasp of structure, and also you're aware of how that structure can be bent – which is something that I was always very interested in, because, to me, experiment for experiment's sake is kind of self-indulgent. If I'm experimenting, it's for a reason. I want to see if a certain effect works. I want to see if it's got, perhaps, further application. So I'd always be very ready to accept any new twist or turn or variation that I could put upon the material to keep it fresh, and to keep it evolving. To keep my sense of story and storytelling as an evolving, living thing.

So when, on *V for Vendetta*, David Lloyd suggested that we do without thought balloons, and do without author's voice captions, and do without sound effects, at first I was horrified, because I thought this was two or three of my favorite crutches being kicked away from me. But, after I'd been doing *V for Vendetta* for a few episodes, I found out what a difference it made to the tone and quality of the story. All of a sudden it made everything much more real and documentary. The less that you relied upon captions and thought balloons, the more compellingly real the dialogue and pictures became. Which I took a stage further with *From Hell*, where we did without any sort of captions at all. Not just did without author's voice captions, but where we never had any internal monologues or anything. And you start to learn something about what effects are appropriate to what sort of story, what sort of thinking is appropriate, and you start to learn some of the real secrets of creativity. Which is "How do you come up with new ideas?" New ideas for stories, new ideas for telling a story.

One of the best analogies I've ever heard was from a book by Douglas R. Hofstadter, the author of *Gödel, Escher, Bach*, and this is a book called, I think, *Metamagical Themas*. It's a collection of his essays, and one of the essays is talking about creativity, and he gives a really nice little example. He says that the way he understands it, is that any situation, any thing, any story, has certain parameters, certain things that make it what it is. If you twist those parameters a little bit, then it will turn into something else. And he said that <u>that</u> is what he saw a lot of creativity being – just twisting

V For Vendetta ™ & © 2005 DC Comics

"So when, on V for Vendetta, David Lloyd suggested that we do without thought balloons and do without sound effects, at first I was horrified"

these knobs which adjust the parameters of the situation. As an example of simple, everyday creativity, he gave the example of a friend of his who'd been a restaurant with his wife. And the friend, noticing the restaurant was crowded, said, "Boy, I'd sure hate to be a waitress in here tonight." And then he said what his friend had done was twisted two knobs on the situation. The first knob was that, instead of a customer at the restaurant in question, he had imagined what it would be like if instead he was an employee. And then, probably for various socio-sexual reasons, he had also switched his gender so he is no longer a male customer, he is now a female employee.

Now that's just a very small example, but it does make Hofstadter's point that this *is* a creative act. This guy has basically, by twisting some of the knobs, if you like, adjusted a few of the parameters of the existing situation and, in doing so, has *created* a new, imaginary situation. Now what Hofstadter was saying was that maybe all creativity's like that to a degree. That, oh, I don't know, you're looking at *Romeo and Juliet* and you suddenly think, "Hey, if you were to twist the knob of time and the knob of place, and have this happen in America in the 1940s or 50s, then bingo! you've got *West Side Story*." That's a pretty easy example, and a pretty obvious one, but what Hofstadter was saying was that maybe what we call geniuses are the people who are twisting the parameter knobs that are so big and deep and fundamental that other people haven't noticed them, haven't even thought maybe you *could* twist *that* idea. People who think, "Yeah, that's just an idea. That's a variable, the same as anything else, maybe you could tamper with that?" Those are the big creative leaps that people make, when they twist a knob that nobody had noticed before. And the effect can be marvelous, you know?

I suppose, one thing in summary of all this, it *pays* to think about your own creativity. One way we do progress is by being conscious of how we operate, how we work. Don't be afraid to *examine* your own creativity. It isn't like riding a bike. It isn't so that, if you actually stopped and thought about how your feet are actually moving around on the pedals, if you stopped and thought about that, you would fall off. Yeah, that's true. Creativity isn't like that. I think that some people have a superstition that if they examine their own creativity, because it is such a wonderful, supernatural thing, and they don't know where it comes from, if they stop to examine it, it'll dry up. It'll all fall to bits. It will stop. The muse will go away. No, that's not it. It's more like driving a car. If you drive a car for a living, you would at least want to know what to do if it suddenly stopped dead. You at least want to have the fundamentals of lifting the hood and tinkering about a little bit and see if you could get it going again.

So I'd say the same thing can be applied to the arts, and to talent in general. *Think* about your processes. *Think* about what you're doing. Is there any reason why you have to do it like that? Why are you doing it like that? What would happen if you did it a different way? What would happen if you varied this, or changed that? Sometimes what would happen would be a disaster, or nothing very interesting. But if you train your mind to at least consider these different oblique angles and possibilities, then that is probably the best way to have a talent which develops, and *continues* to develop, rather than a talent which will reach some point at which it's satisfied with itself, and will then switch off. *Never* be satisfied with what you're doing. Don't be suicidal and morbidly dissatisfied with what you're doing, no need to beat yourself up, but simply admit that you probably could have done it better, and that next time, with a little more thought, a little more ingenuity and inventiveness, you will do it better. And that's the way to progress. That's the way to avoid ending up as some novelists do, in a kind of golden rut. Where, yes, they're still selling lots of books, but their last twenty books have been the same, with changes of character, dialogue, whatever, and the actual thrill of their writing has long since been extinguished. I mean, of course, if you're just in it for the money, then find yourself a golden rut and plow it until you die, with my blessing.

But if you want to be a *writer*, which is about something more than a career, then I'd advise that you be as adventurous as possible, be as thoughtful as possible. Understand some of this strange territory that you are moving over. Understand your own motives, and understand the path that you are taking, and why you are taking that particular path across the terrain, and I think you will be a better writer for it. You might not be a richer writer, you might not be a happier writer, but you'll be a better writer.

BB: I was going to ask this later, but since you've broached the subject, what is a writer in your mind? You've suggested that it's much more than just a career, so what does it mean to be a writer?

AM: To me, as I said, probably at the beginning of our conversation, to me writing is the core of magic, it's the core of consciousness. Now, why do I write? If that's the question, I would say that whatever any of us choose to think, whatever any of us would like to believe, as writers, or as artists, we have a lot in common with Paul Joseph Goebbels. That all art is propaganda. It is not propaganda for the nation state of Germany, it is propaganda for a state of mind. It is a broadcast from each of our lonely little broadcasting stations that sends out a signal -- our impressions. This is how we see the world. This is our worldview. And we probably want people to at least *share* our worldview, if only for the hours that they spend reading the novel, or the minutes they spend reading the comic, we want to *color* their worldview with ours for a little while.

To show them some of the things from inside our mind, our imagination. We probably want to, if we have any opinions upon life and the world, we probably, without dictating, want to at least make these available to other people. Not to force them to think the same thing that we think, see things the same way that we do, but to at least give them the option. And if we believe that the way that we see things is useful, then we would probably want to do our best to represent that worldview as enticingly as possible, to make it as attractive as possible. So we hone our writing skills.

Nobody wants to use the words "mind control," but in some way that is what all art is. [General laughter] If you tell someone a joke, it is mind control. Or at least *attempted* mind control. You're trying to make them laugh. If you tell somebody a tragic story about Little Nell dying of croup on the orphanage steps, then, yeah, that's mind control. That's, in a rather simplistic and sort of offensive way, manipulating people's emotions, crudely and bluntly, to make them weep, to basically move them to tears. Which is very easy to do. All you have to do is show some people a picture of a battered seal pup, and they'll burst into tears. It's not a difficult trick. Whether you *should* do it indiscriminately, just to make people upset, that's a different question.

All of us who are writers, if we've written a scene which we've found sad and moving, we probably would prefer it if the readers found it sad and moving, as well, rather than that the readers were laughing all the way through it. So we use our skills. We use our talents and our techniques to actually *change* the readers' consciousness. To change their mood. To change the way that they perceive a certain issue. And I suppose that, like any individual, whether they're a writer or not, I found myself born into a world which a lot of the time seems to me to be <u>unfair</u> to various people, *painful* to a lot of its inhabitants, *unlivable* to a lot of its inhabitants, and I would *prefer* it if that were not the case. I would prefer it if nobody hurt.

Now, I'm not likely to get my preference, you know? In fact, a world in which nobody hurt is almost completely unimaginable. But if I could do anything to raise the level of the debate; if I've found any headway with certain issues and can make that information available to other people; if I can, in some small way, perhaps make things better for a couple of readers, then that is added, by some tiny measure, to the balance of human pleasure of the world, as opposed to human pain, or to information as opposed to ignorance. This is not to say that any writer can go out and change the world with a single book. Maybe they could, if it's *Mein Kampf*, or something like that. But if you're a published writer, and you've had even a couple of thousand people read what you do, the chances are that, even if it's only a point of a percentage, that at least one of those people will have had some sort of elevating experience.

And <u>that</u> does feel good. When readers come up to you, years later, and say, "This book saved my life," "This book made me leave home," "This book lead me into a career of crime," or whatever, when you can think, "Yes, I made a difference to this incarcerated person who's talking to me now," you actually feel that your words, your thoughts, have some form of interaction with the world. Yes, it's going to be a long time before you see any improvements in the world as a result of your efforts. You'll probably *never* see any improvement in the world. But for my part, I chose to believe that it is the sum of all of these efforts, by all of these people, across all of these years that have kept us, as a species, rolling ever-so-slowly forward.

So I suppose that being a writer, being a creative individual is, to me, an attempt to put my shoulder to the wheel and justify my costly existence upon this planet. I'll probably eat more than my fair share of the planet's food, take up more than my fair share of its space, all of this stuff, you know?

I would like it if I was at least giving something back, if I was providing something to people out there that might, in some way, alleviate their situation, give them a different point of view upon it, whatever. I'm sure that in 90% of the readers' cases, or 98%, I fail miserably. But for that 2%, that has an effect. And that is what I do it for.

BB: OK. Well, jumping back to the topic of creativity, and the real meat of our subject, do you consciously choose properties and topics, or do they seem to suggest themselves to you?

AM: Well, it depends. It depends from work to work. The first series that I did, there were vague editorial suggestions made about things.

When I was doing *Warrior*, then I think Dez Skinn originally wanted a 1930s noir detective thriller type strip for me and Dave Lloyd to work on. So I accepted that brief. I would do a strip that Dave Lloyd could enjoy working on, and it'd have all the elements of 1930s noir. But Dave Lloyd said that he didn't want to do it any more. He'd just finished doing a run on the *Nightraven* strip, which had meant lots of reference work looking up 1930s cars, and he really didn't want to do that again.

So I tried to analyze what it was about 30s noir detective strips that made them so appealing. And I thought, "Well, setting them in the 30s means that it's still a close enough time in history so that, more or less, everything is still recognizable. The people are dressed in clothing that's quite like ours. All right, there's a quaintness to the cars and the buildings and the fashions, but this is still recognizably our world -- just a few decades ago. Could that be transferred to the near future from the near past, maintaining the same effect? Where you've got a world that's recognizably like ours, so that we can identify with it, but different enough to be romantic and exotic." You know, the 1930s is close enough to our time to be recognizable, but far enough away to be exotic. If we were to leap a few decades into the future, still recognizably our times, but having progressed to a completely different situation, would that still work? And it was from there that *V for Vendetta* evolved, from that idea.

With *Swamp Thing*, Len Wein phoned up and said, "How would you like to write *Swamp Thing*?" And I just said, "Sure," because my basic philosophy at that time was that, if I actually wanted to make it as a working writer, the best thing to do was to accept any project, and then find a way to make it interesting to work on.

I'd already made the decision that I would not write anything that I did not enjoy writing; I would not just hack stuff out, because if I was going to do that, I might as well go into advertising. If I was going to write something, I would have to be interested in at least some element of it. And so what this meant in practice, if anybody asked me if I wanted to do anything, I would say, "Yes," and then, even if it was something that I had no interest in at all, I would try and devise

Snakes and Ladders©2001 Alan Moore and
Eddie Campbell

"We use our talents and our
techniques to change the readers'
consciousness."

a way to *make* it interesting to me. I mean, Swamp Thing was a great character when Len Wein and Bernie Wrightson were doing him back in the 1970s, but there were a lot of decent characters around. I hadn't really had any special thoughts about Swamp Thing. But having the idea put to me, then I started to, first, dissect the idea to see what Swamp Thing is all about, what bits of the strip *are* promising, or do hold the spark of interesting ideas, what bits are limiting the strips, holding it back. What is it that doesn't work about Swamp Thing in his current incarnation? And I kind of prepared maybe ten pages, or something, of a kind of treatise, a critique of Swamp Thing. What I thought had potential about the character, what I thought was limiting it. I sent this in, the people at DC seemed quite impressed by my reasoning, and I then put those ideas into application on the *Swamp Thing* series.

With strips that I've created myself from scratch, like *Watchmen* ... I don't know. They tend to grow out of the situations. I think what *Watchmen* grew out of was just the opportunity to do an extended project with Dave Gibbons. And we went through various different possibilities; a Challengers of the Unknown strip, a Martian Manhunter strip. If any of those had been picked up on, then there probably wouldn't have been a *Watchmen*, which came from our Charlton heroes idea. And, eventually, what seemed viable was what turned into *Watchmen*. What provides the germ of an idea can come from anywhere.

With *From Hell*, for a number of years, a couple of years at least, I'd been thinking about writing something about a murder. It struck me that a murder was a complex human event, but that murder stories, murder fiction, tended to simplify things into a whodunit where, once you knew who'd done it, what they'd done it with, and why they'd done it, that was the whole case solved, that was the whole concluded. Whereas, in Northampton, for some reason we do have a much higher murder rate, per capita, than a lot of far larger and more notorious places in England. So, yeah, you live here long enough and, if you're lucky, there'll be a murder round the corner. If you're not lucky, it'll be you. [General laughter] But, eventually, you'll meet a murderer or two, or one will happen a couple of streets down. And when you have any knowledge of <u>real</u> murders, you see it's not all "Professor Plum in the conservatory with the lead pipe." It's about what *happens* in communities, in people's lives, in families. What *happens* in the vortex around the murder.

The *murder* is generally an event of about forty five seconds duration that usually happens when people are drunk, or in some other extreme state. The actual murder itself is not a very complex event. You know, somebody gets drunk, hits somebody else around the head with a baseball bat a few times, and they're dead. There's not much to that. But all of the tensions that lead up to it, all of the things in the lives of those people, all of the various social threads that lead into and out of the murder, they're fascinating. There is a lot to understand *there*. And it was these general musings that eventually lead me to *From Hell*.

At first, I dismissed the idea of Jack the Ripper as having been done to death and being too played out. Later, I took another look at the case and realized that, yeah, there was a way that I could write about the Jack the Ripper story in a way that *hadn't* been done before, and which would enable me to explore the things that <u>I</u> wanted to explore about a murder. Sometimes it will be an abstract idea like that, where I've not got any particular story that I want to tell, but where it will strike me that, if I was going to write a murder story, say, I wouldn't do it in a style of a whodunit. So, how would I do it? And that kind of thought leads to *From Hell*.

I had similar thoughts about sex comics and pornography. For a number of years I'd thought, "Why is it that almost <u>every</u> part of human activity -- being a cowboy, or a detective, or a space explorer, even if very few of us actually do these things in real life -- it has it's own genre down at the book shops. Whereas all of us have a sexual identity, and yet the only genre that's devoted to sex is this grubby, ugly, under-the-counter genre that has absolutely no standards, moral, aesthetic or otherwise, and therefore seems likely to remain as a grubby, ugly, under-the-counter genre. And

I've often thought, "Why is that so?" Why Is It that we can see *spectacularly* inventive acts of violence, and yet even fairly ordinary, non-inventive acts of sex are proscribed to us? Why do no serious artists ever want to bring their talents to the field of sex? Are they embarrassed? Could it be done? Could you write a piece of pornography that was beautiful, that was intelligent, and was loving, and had all of the things that you'd expect an ordinary novel or work of art to have, but was just horny and about sex? Is that possible?

These kind of abstract musings eventually lead to *Lost Girls*, which we're just finishing at the moment. Me and Melinda [Gebbie], we've been working on it, I think, for about twelve years, thirteen years, and she's just on the last chapter at the moment. And I think it will have done what we set out to do. We'll have provided a book that is pornographic in that it <u>is</u> arousing, and it *intends* to arouse, because that's the job that pornography has to do. If it's not arousing, then it isn't erotic, it isn't pornography. At the same time, we have tried to do something which is accessible to both men <u>and</u> women, something that is <u>not</u> morally ugly, that is intelligent, that has characters, that has a plot, that has a theme, that has motifs. That has all of these fancy literary things that you'd expect to find in a <u>proper</u> book, but it's in a sex book. And, yeah, that purely sprang out of abstract musings. You know, "What is it about pornography ...?" "What is it about murder stories ...?" "What do I like, what don't I like?" *That* can be the seed of a story. They come from different places.

Like the ABC characters, for example. *There's* a spooky little story. [General laughter] When Rob Liefeld's Awesome/Extreme Comics went under, and I found that both myself and, more importantly, a number of the artists that I had been working with were suddenly without a regular gig, I thought, "Hm, maybe I should perhaps try and come up with a raft of titles. A nice little self-contained comics line that we could maybe do something good with." So that seemed like a workable idea, so I was trying to think of what comics I might want to do. And I was looking through one of my innumerable, messy work books that I've filled

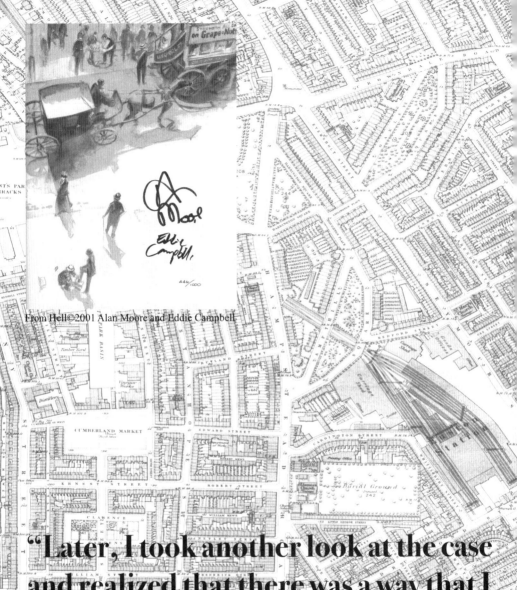

From Hell ©2001 Alan Moore and Eddie Campbell

"Later, I took another look at the case and realized that there was a way that I could write about Jack the Ripper in a way that hadn't been done before"

with scribbles, doodles, pages in completely the wrong sequence of whatever books I'm working on at the time, laid out in rough diagram form, bits of dialogue, and in one of these, on an otherwise blank page I found a list of names that I'd written perhaps one night when I was just oddly musing and trying to think up what would be good character names. I don't remember, I don't remember writing these things.

But there in a list I had Tom Strong, Cobweb, Promethea, Grey Shirt, Jack B. Quick, and a couple of others. Just a little list in the middle of the page, for no reason at all, there were these names. And I thought, "Yeah, one night I must have been sitting there just trying to think of cool names for comic characters that didn't sound like the kind of names that were around at present." So, yeah, I just took those names and turned them into the ABC line. There were no notes upon who Tom Strong or Promethea were, I had to just take the names and then think, "What sort of guy would have a name like this? What sort of strip might could grow out of this name?" So, yeah, the genesis for Tom Strong or Promethea was just a simple one or two words on a piece of paper. Simply a name, and everything grew from there.

A story can grow from anything. I think what you have to develop is the *eye* to *spot* what is a promising or viable possible story. To discriminate. To be able to see, from an early stage, which ones are going to be able to go the distance, which ones are maybe not as good as they might have been.

Some ideas you can just tell. I mean, when I had the idea for *League of Extraordinary Gentlemen*, I knew straight away that this was a top drawer idea. Because it was *blindingly* obvious, *blindingly* simple, and nobody had done it. Those are always the best. The *best* ideas are the simplest "Why didn't anybody think of that before?" ideas, you know? It's just a matter of learning to recognize them, I guess.

BB: You work in a number of media these days. You perform, you do music, you write lyrics and poetry and novels and comics. Now, we've been mainly discussing comics, which leads to the question of whether the idea dictates the format?

AM: Well, what you're doing, what the idea is for ... To some degree the format dictates the idea. All right, Eddie Campbell turned *The Birth Caul* and *Snakes and Ladders*, these are both performances, *he* turned them into comic books. They were not *intended* as comic books. If I'd been trying to think of a comic book to do with Eddy, I would never have written *The Birth Caul*, I would never have written *Snakes and Ladders*. The reason they turned out how they did was because I had been given a specific invitation to come up with a certain sort of performance, words and music, at these specific events. And knowing that this was material to be read aloud made a difference to how I put the words together. Knowing that my audience was going to be very, very different to the audience in comics made me aware that I could explore broader themes, perhaps more mature or progressive themes than the comic audience will usually stand still for. So the possibilities of the format, of the actual medium, *they* more than anything determined how the work came out. I think it's more like that than the other way around.

  Like I say, even though Eddy did a *brilliant* job and made both *The Birth Caul* and *Snakes and Ladders* work as really, *really* good comics, that's more down to Eddy. I'd got no idea of producing them as comics at that stage. They were simply performances and then, shortly thereafter, the idea of making a permanent record with a CD, those were my only considerations. And, yeah, the fact that it was a different audience, a different medium entirely, *that* probably influenced the content, rather than the other way around. It's not like I had the idea for *The Birth Caul* and then thought, "How shall I do this?" It was, "We've got a performance to do. What shall we do for the performance?" And it was largely that way around, rather than the reverse.

BB: What about structure? Again, it's something that's incredibly

Important to your work, so I was wondering if, depending on the project, that's something you *assign* to it, or if you tend to *find* it, *discover* it, within the piece?

AM: Different ways of doing it. Sometimes you can impose a structure, sometimes you can find a structure. And this depends upon where I am in my working life. Back when I was starting out, I was a *fetishist* for structure, I think. I wanted to know where every last nut and bolt was going before I'd start the story. If it was an issue of *Swamp Thing*, then I'd have the numbers 1 through 24 down the side of the page, to represent the twenty-four pages, and then I'd have a little synopsis written besides each number of what had got to happen on that page. And sometimes I'd spend a long time writing and rewriting that simple page order, until I'd got a structure that I'd knew would work. If I was doing something ambitious, like, for example, the abortive *Big Numbers*, for that I had one of the most frightening pieces of structure that you have ever seen. [General laughter]
  It was a huge sheet of A-1 paper, which is the largest paper size over here. I'm not sure if you have the same measurements over there, but this is a *huge* piece of paper. It's sort of a map. Across the top, it was divided into twelve columns – down, vertically, it was divided into twelve columns. And then it was divided down the side horizontally, where it had got the names of about forty-eight characters. And so the whole thing became a grid of tiny, little boxes, that each contained what that character would be doing in that issue. So it was in tiny, tiny little writing that looked like it had been done by a mental patient. It was frightening to look at. I mean, one of the main reasons I did it was to frighten other writers. [General laughter] Just for the look on Neil Gaiman's face, you know. But I was aware that with *Big Numbers* I was doing something much more complex and more abstract than I'd ever done before, and I wanted it to be absolutely water-tight in it's structure. So, that's how I used to work then, fifteen years ago.
  But, like with *From Hell*, I knew the whole Jack the Ripper story,

and I saw what kind of time period it took place over, and I worked out that I would need sixteen chapters – well, fourteen chapters, a prologue and an epilogue – in order to tell the whole story. How long those chapters would be, I didn't know, and I didn't want to fix. I wanted to give myself room. I knew that new information would turn up in the course of researching the book. I wanted to leave myself room to put it in. So, yeah, it was going to be sixteen chapters, but some of those chapters would be eight to twelve pages, some of them would be sixty pages. So that was the beginning of a kind of flexibility that I allowed myself.

With the ABC books, it's riding bareback, you know? I had ideas for characters, and I'd got very little idea of what the characters were going to be doing – right up until when I wrote the first issues. And if I'm writing an issue of an ABC book these days, I'll probably just think, "What would be a good opening scene?" and then, "How to follow that?" I like to try to leave it open and fresh. There's something thrilling about working without a safety net. Given twenty-five years of experience in this business, I'm pretty good at pulling myself out of jams, you know? Or, better still, not getting into them in the first place. So I don't really need to be absolutely certain of the structure of a story, or where a story's going, when I've started. I'm confident that will *emerge* as the story progresses, and that keeps it fresher for me.

You know, I think there is a sort of freshness about the ABC comics that, yeah, given my work up to that point, I think the ABC works seem quite fresh and lively. And that was probably because I wouldn't be working out a whole Jack B. Quick story, I'd be thinking, "What would be a really stupid first panel for a Jack B. Quick story? Oh, yeah, Schrödinger's Cat! He's trying to get a cat into a box, and he's saying something funny. Yeah, that'll do. That's a good first panel." Although now I'm stuck with a story about Jack B. Quick and cats, you know, so I'll have to work out something that carries on from there. And we got that nice little Jack B. Quick "buttered cat" story out of it. It was just springing into the void, and trusting that you'd grow a parachute before you hit

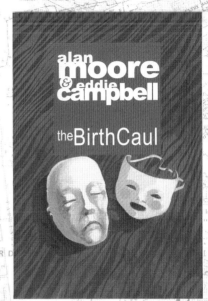

The Birth Caul©1999 Alan Moore and
Eddie Campbell Comics

"The fact that it was a different audience, a different medium entirely,
that probably influenced the content,
rather than the other way around"

rock bottom, I think.

That's the kind of technique I'm using at the moment. A lot more spontaneous, and sort of fresher. But give it another year, and I could be drawing complex and arcane charts again and all the rest of it. It's basically what feels best at the time. The processes tend to suggest themselves.

BB: How important is research to your work?

AM: It didn't use to be important at all, because I had a morbid dread of it. I really didn't want to have to do any work, that sounded too much like being back at school.

Probably one of the first things that I did that involved a lot of research was *Brought to Light*, which I did with Joyce Brabner, where the Christic Institute sent me a mass of books, they sent me their affidavit for the court case, so that I could see their entire court case with dates, and names, and sums of money, and all the rest of it. And that was very daunting when I looked at all that stuff, the pile of paperbacks that I was going to have to read.

But the intellectual puzzle of being able to put together a history of CIA covert operations since the end of the second World War, that touched upon all the things that this affidavit touched upon, and to get all that into thirty pages, when you don't even know if it's possible to do that, *that* was real fun. [General laughter] It was such a logistical nightmare, you know? And to do it in a way that it *wouldn't* be dry as dust, to do it in a way where it would grip the readers' imagination, even if you *were* just giving endless facts about shady meetings, briefcases full of money, surprising deaths, wars, coups, drug deals; to try and make it grip the reader, that was a logistical problem. And it did give me a taste for it.

For one thing, the stuff you get from research is real life. And so it's usually much stranger than fiction, and it has details that you just simply could not invent. *Wonderful* little details. And after having done *Brought to Light*, and also the piece that I did for AARGH – the Artists Against Rampant Government Homophobia, the benefit book that we did when they brought in the anti-gay legislation in Britain in the late 1980s – and I wrote a piece for that that was a very compact history of gay culture. Which I was surprised to find that ...

With that, I assumed I could just go down to the local book shop, and there'd be a history of gay culture there on the shelf and I could just take it down and read through it. I found, shamefully perhaps, that there was no coherent and broad history of gay culture that existed in any form. And I believe, from what I've heard, there's still very little on those lines that exist today, which is why Jose Villarrubia is currently turning what was an eight page poem in the original AARGH into an eighty page book.

Because there's an authority that comes with researched material. If you've researched it, if you're sure of it, then there's a tone of authority that fills your voice. You're sure of your facts, and it fills the story, you know?

Before doing massively researched things like that, I suppose that my only exposure to research would be like, say, when they asked me to do *Swamp Thing*, and I'd never been to America. I asked where *Swamp Thing* was set, and we came up with the swamps of Louisiana as the best option. So I thought, "Right, let's find out about Louisiana, because otherwise I'm going to be making all sorts of horrible mistakes." So I went and read up about Louisiana. I found out about the music. I found out about the slang. I found out about the cooking. I found out about the history. I looked it up in road maps and things like that, and tried to get a feel for the place and talk about it authentically. And it turned out I was probably talking about it in greater authentic detail than most of the American writers who'd been on the strip. Well, I suppose, perhaps to Americans, they wouldn't really feel the need to research Louisiana, because it's a commonplace kind of location to them. Whereas, because I was more uncertain of getting it right, I really researched it and came up with what I think was a – this is, of course, helped greatly by Steve Bissette and John Totleben and Rick Veitch and all the other artists on the book – I think what we created between us was very authentically textured Louisiana. Perhaps it's not the real Louisiana, but it certainly allowed the readers to suspend disbelief for twenty-four pages. So, that's another way in which reference can be useful.

I suppose I would say, you don't want to over do it. *Don't* wear your reference on your sleeve, you know? So try and make it look as casual as possible. Because if you fall in love with your reference so much that you want to advertise it in every word balloon that you write, then that probably won't come across that well. You have to use moderation. Research something to death? By all means. But be sparing in which pieces of your reference you choose to highlight, or choose to include. There's a lot to be said for the *telling* detail, rather than acres of regurgitated, if knowledgeable, reference.

These days, I actually love the process of doing reference work. Doing the almanac for the second book of *League of Extraordinary Gentlemen*, it's a hell of a lot of work researching all that, but, by the time we're finished, we'll have near enough the whole globe of fiction completely mapped. And that fills me with such great satisfaction, that we could have the whole planet of fiction circumscribed and mapped within fifty pages. That's marvelous. I wouldn't have thought that we could do that, but we could.

BB: How do you keep track of all of this information? Do you keep it all in your head, in your notebooks, or a combination of the two?

AM: My actual writing is down in the notebooks. Like today there are four rectangles, with scribbly pictures in the rectangles, and then there are lots of numbered bursts of dialogue or captions in the rest of the area on the page. This is pages 8 through 11 of *Promethea* #24. I've typed that up. When I go back to *Promethea* in a day or two's time, I shall read through it again, and then carry on.

No, I don't keep notes. I keep it all in my head. Like, at the moment I'm finding it difficult to remember exactly how *many* strips I'm doing, let alone what they are. But that's just temporary. I'm a

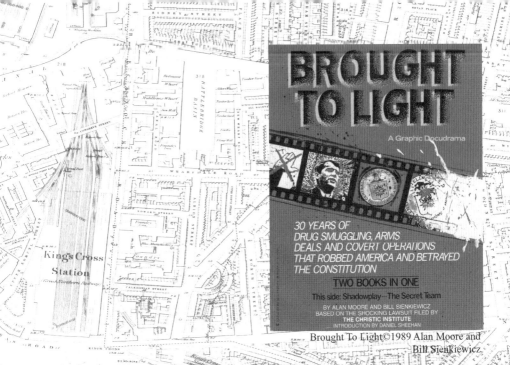

Brought To Light ©1989 Alan Moore and
Bill Sienkiewicz.

"The intellectual puzzle of being able to put together a history of CIA operations since the second World War into thirty pages, that was real fun"

bit overloaded at the moment. But, yeah, I keep it all in my head. I've got a pretty scary memory, you know? Never forget a grudge. [General laughter] And I remember quite trivial things from quite long ago, so I don't keep notes.

I'd advise any writer to keep a commonplace book. But my commonplace book is in my head, and it doesn't let me down that much. So, no, I don't really keep notes as to where I am, or even when the deadline is, or anything like that. I find I can generally rely upon memory and instinct.

BB: OK. It sounds like you're still starting out creating the strips in longhand, in these notebooks.

AM: Yep, absolutely. It's all in longhand. I use a word processor, which means I *do* own a computer. I'm told I *could* connect up to the Internet with this. I got no desire to, or, indeed, to do anything with the computer other than use it as a glorified typewriter, and it has a fax machine attached to it.

Well, if I'm doing prose. If I'm doing say a prose introduction, like recently I've done an introduction to a new Michael Moorcock book, and I wanted to do a well-written introduction, so I spent a few days on it. And I wrote that straight at the typewriter. That involves just as much sitting and scratching my head and not touching the keyboard for a half hour while I get round a tricky sentence or something, and then I'll have a sudden burst of increased flow and there'll be a couple of paragraphs that pour out. And, yeah, I'll compose bits of prose that way.

Some of the performance pieces have been partly composed straight at the keyboard, but *generally* everything is done with a biro and scraps of paper. There is just something that I really like about the convenience and control of a simple notepad and pencil. There's something so basic about it. There's not many parts to go wrong, you know?

So, yeah, more or less everything's written longhand first.

46

BB: And you also work out the comics page and layout visually, right?

AM: Oh yeah. Well, with the comics, I have these little rectangles that I mentioned earlier with *Promethea*, that have the scribbly drawings in, these scribbly drawings you wouldn't even want to call them thumbnails, unless they're particularly damaged thumbnails, because they're not really comprehensible to anybody but me. I know that this little blob down in the lower left corner of a panel, with a couple of odd squiggles attached to it, is actually a head and shoulders shot of character A, who is facing away from us towards the right background, where character B is standing in a full figure shot, gesturing with his hands as he says this or that or the other. This is a tiny little thing, much smaller than a postage stamp, with a couple of squiggles in it. But *I* know what it's *meant* to be.

So then, when I sit and go to the typewriter, I can then transform these incomprehensible scribbles into quite lavish and detailed panel descriptions which will not only tell you where characters A and B are in the panel, but will also tell you what they're wearing, what the lighting is like, what the room that they are in is like, the exact angle of the shot, the expressions on their faces, the kind of body language that they have. Which is nothing that I could ever convey in a drawing, no matter how detailed I was doing it. So with words I can convey all that, and then leave it up to the artists.

So, yeah, with comics, there are always page layouts that I'm doing. The artists might change them, but that's up to them. And I give the artists the *freedom* to change them, because my ideas might not always be the most inspired. But my ideas will work as a basic place to start from, or to fall back upon. If they *can't* think of anything better, my way of doing it will work. If they *can* think of something better, that improves upon my way of doing it, then that's great. That makes me look good. But if they're not having a particularly inspired day, if they just follow my instructions, we'll get a good story out of it.

If you're a comic writer, you *have* to think of the pictures, you *have* to think visually. It's no good just thinking in terms of words and situations, you have to think in terms of images. And even if, like me, you're not a particularly good artist, then there's nothing wrong with just putting down meaningless scribbles, as long as they have meaning to you, as long as you know that the picture would work if drawn like that. So, yeah, with the comic work, there's loads and loads of drawings.

BB: Was one of the reasons behind your move from a typewriter to the computer the ease with which you can do rewrites using the word processor?

AM: *Slightly*, but you have to understand that anything you've ever read of mine was probably a first draft. I don't do rewrites because ... God, that's boring! [General laughter] It's generally been such a grind writing the thing in the first place, that the idea of rewriting it is a nightmare. Also, if I was a novelist, and I get to chapter eight and suddenly realize that there was something that I wanted to include back in chapter one, I could do that. But if you're a comic writer, then by the time you're up to chapter eight, chapter one has already been published for about three months. The deadlines are very fast and furious, you haven't really got time to do multiple rewrites on a story, and it's not possible to go back and amend or fine tune earlier chapters, so you have to try and develop a style of getting it right the first time, or making as few mistakes as possible.

   The thing with a word processor is that it makes it easier to do corrections as I go along. I don't have to paint correction fluid over the word in question, wait 'til it dries, go back and type over it. Which I always used to do until I actually got a word processor. So, yeah, being able to do all of that electronically, that's a boon. That saves a lot of messing about.

   But I don't really do rewrites. If I did, I'm sure that would be very handy, as well. But it's, more or less, it's all first draft. It's all pretty much fresh as it comes out of my head, what you see on the page.

"I have these scribby drawings that you wouldn't even want to call them thumbnails because they're not really comprehensible to anyone but me"

BB: Is that true with the performance pieces and the novel, as well?

AM: The performance pieces, yes, that's true. Because, again, generally I'll never leave myself enough time to do the performance pieces. All of the performance pieces have been written, and the music has been composed and recorded and mixed, within two weeks. That's the whole album. The words of the whole album have also been written in about two weeks. So the whole album takes about a fortnight to do.

I don't know if you've heard any of the performance pieces, but in terms of albums, musically *and* lyrically, they are a lot more dense and complex than anything else you're going to get out there. I'm not saying *better*, but more dense and complex. It certainly doesn't take us five years to do an album like the Stone Roses, you know?

So we do them very quickly. It's a very intense process because taking two weeks to write an hour's worth of material, it is quite quick, but then it's quite slow, as well. You know, you're spending every day you can afford to working on it. I don't have to rewrite a sentence, because I've maybe spent ten minutes, a quarter of an hour, an hour writing it in the first place. I've been very careful.

On the novel, the first eleven chapters were pretty much exactly as they were when I first wrote them, other than a word here or there that got changed. The last chapter is the only thing that I've ever done a rewrite on, I think. In that I was anxious to get it in by my deadline, and I kind of rushed it. It was a tricky chapter anyway, and my editor, Faith Brooker, said she wasn't sure about it, and would I like to have another go at it? And I thought that she was probably right. There was stuff about it that dissatisfied me, so I went back and rewrote it. And, yeah, the second version was an awful lot better. That was the right version, you know?

But that's the only chapter of the novel that I rewrote, and that's about the only thing that I've rewritten out of my entire career, apart some of those early stories to *2000AD*, where Alan Grant would make suggestions. But I was starting out. I expected to do a lot of rewrites then. These days, no, I expect to get it right the first time.

I've been doing it long enough, I *should* be able to get it right the first time by now.

BB: Also, you've put a great deal of thought into it, beforehand.

AM: Yeah, that's it. I mean, I'm a big boy now, so I ought to be able to do it like that.
    So that's pretty much how I work. It is pretty much first draft. But it's a very *deliberate* and *deliberated over* first draft.

BB: Have you had much reason to redialogue stuff after seeing what the artist has put on the page?

AM: Uhm, no, not really. In fact, never.
    Perhaps with the other people, it would be where the writer has only given the very barest description of the page in question. The Marvel style – what used to be called Marvel style comics writing – where you'd have, say, "Pages ten to twelve, these two characters fight", and you'd have it broken down like that, and then the artists would do most of the actual storytelling, and then it would go back to the writer for the dialoguing. Now, the artist does not know what kind of dialogue these people are going to be saying. If the writer has suggested that they be included on the page, he'll know that they're perhaps saying something, but he won't know what. And that's when you tend to get those kind of neutral expressions, so that he doesn't look sad, he doesn't look happy, he looks kind of serious, maybe a bit constipated. It's kind of neutral.
    But, with the way that I write stories, where I'm explaining what a character's face looks like, what kind of emotions are registering upon it, their body language, everything like that, then me and the artist are very much on the same page, you know? No, I've almost never had to re-do dialogue.
    The *only* time when I had to re-do dialogue – and this wasn't the artist's fault, it was probably mine – it was that issue of *Promethea*, issue # 15, where we did that Mobius strip spread. Which, yeah,

my mother used to tell me that I was far too clever for my own good, and that it would only lead me into trouble, and I should have listened to her. But I thought, "Yeah, this'll be cool. We'll do this Mobius strip and it'll drive the readers mad just trying to follow the dialogue around." And then I spent ten pages actually describing that page to Jim [J. H. Williams]...

Normally it's probably about, for every page of comic that you read, I have written about two pages of script. Generally. Sometimes three. With that particular spread of *Promethea*, just two pages of the actual comic, the actual script describing it was ten pages long. Which is well over the top, even for me. And I was trying to describe this Mobius strip, and the figures of Barbara and Sophie as they walked around it, so that it'd be saying, "Now in this first panel, at the top we've got figures of Barbara and Sophie moving from left to right down the slope, and they look like this. And then, *under* them, upside down, we have some other figures of Barbara and Sophie that are moving in the opposite direction. And then down at the bottom, we have some more figures of Barbara and Sophie, and then *under* that bit of the strip, we have another upside down Barbara and Sophie ..." And I'd go through the whole two pages like that.

Somehow, in these over-complex panel directions, me and Jim had a misunderstanding. I'd asked for a Mobius strip, and what I've got laid out on my roughs was a Mobius strip. Jim had *drawn* a Mobius strip, but it didn't *twist* in the same place that mine did. And so, consequently, when Todd [Klein] had come to letter it, he'd done his best, bless him, but something had gone horribly wrong and it no longer made a *shred* of sense. So what I did was ...

I couldn't ask Jim to do the art work again, because it was such a beautiful piece of art work, and it would be much easier for me, well, I spent a few hours doing it, but I went through and redialogued it. We still had at least one mistake in the comic, but I've corrected it again for the third volume of the hardback [collections], and the version in there is absolutely right.

So, no, I've never had to rewrite dialogue because the artist has shown people looking differently or acting differently or doing different things. It was a technical problem when we were doing a technically very complex little set piece in that particular issue. So, no, I've never had any complaints at all with the way any of the artists working on my strips have realized them. I've been very lucky. Nearly everybody that I've ever worked with has always given me their absolute best, and you can't ask for better than that.

BB: That brings us to another interesting question, which is what do you look for in your artists?

AM: Slave-like devotion. [General laughter] No. What I look for in my artists is ...

Before I work with them, if possible, I look at their work and I try to work out what they like to draw. What really spins their prop. And then I will write a strip which will play to what I perceive as their strengths. Even if these might be strengths which they, themselves, have not perceived.

It's like, doing *Lost Girls*, I know Melinda's art work very well, and I constructed the scenes so that Melinda can show off all the many things that she does excellently.

When I was writing *From Hell*, I was very much aware of Eddie's style, and what it could be used for. The same with writing *Watchmen*. I was aware of Dave Gibbons with this meticulous surveyor's eye for detail that he brings to everything, and what that meant in terms of story possibilities. That we could get all of these finely textured details into the backgrounds of the panels, tell a whole other story that was going on in the details. So it's more a matter of me tuning myself to the artist, rather than looking for something specific in the artist. When I *have* had an idea for a strip, and *then* had an idea for the artist ...

Like with *League of Extraordinary Gentlemen*, I had the idea for the strip. Kevin [O'Neil] didn't strike me as the likeliest choice immediately, but as soon as I'd *had* the idea, it was the *only* idea.

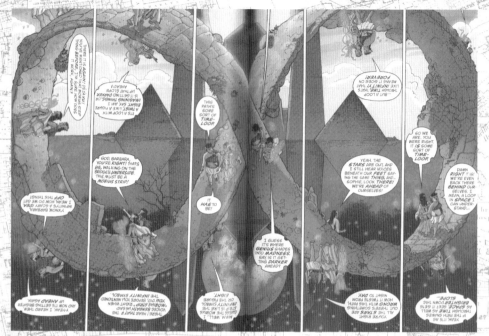

"Jim [Williams] had drawn a Mobius strip, but it didn't twist in the same place that mine did"

I don't know what I'd have done if he had said, "No." I phoned up and said, "Look, Kev, I've got this idea for a strip. I think it'd be really cool. Are you doing anything at the minute? Would you fancy a crack at it?" And Kevin liked the idea. It was just something about when I was coming up with the basic idea for *League of Extraordinary Gentlemen*, I thought, "This really needs a kind of an *extreme* artist who's got a brilliant imagination for design, and who's got ..." I don't know. I don't know what the qualities were that I was looking for. I think "Kevin O'Neil" would best sum up the qualities that I was looking for.

With Eddie Campbell, when he was suggested, he struck me immediately as, "Yeah. That is the *perfect* person to do this possibly very bloody and gory comic strip," because Eddie, his art work, at least in terms of its horror value, is incredibly understated. Which I think is what gave *From Hell* so much of its punch. That it's understated, and when the horror happens, it happens in a completely credible, everyday world. And, yeah, which Eddie is the perfect artist to realize and bring to life.

So different horses for different courses, and generally I will be writing ... It's sort of circus horses dancing to the band. The horses aren't dancing to the band, the band are playing along with the prancing of the horses. And that's kind of how I do my comic strips. I *know* what the artists are good at, I *know* what they like drawing, and I kind of try and play the music to suit that. And it comes out looking very integrated. Someone said of *From Hell* that it looked like the work of one person, which I think both me and Eddie were immensely flattered by. Because I like the thought that I *do* work well with other people, you know? It's like dancing: You know when to lead, you know when to follow. If you can do it elegantly, that's great. That's great.

BB: What's your typical work day like?

AM: There isn't one. Like, today. Let's see ...
I got up. Melinda Gebbie was over, she's over two or three

nights a week, she was over last night. So for a couple of hours I sat around with Melinda and then she went off to do her work, back to her house and look after her things that needed doing. Then I started work on the *Promethea* pages that I'd promised Jim Williams, and there were various phone calls that came while I was writing them, and then when I was typing them. But I got them finished. I probably started them around 11, something like that, and I'd got them typed up by about 3. Four pages, four hours. But that was slow, because there were a lot of phone calls, and interruptions, and things like that. Then, round about 3, I made myself a couple of sandwiches. And then the phone rang. I forget who that was, but that was a quite lengthy sort of conversation. And then I've been picking away at some stuff for *League* # 5, but there's been phone calls ever since, so I'm probably done for today.

I mean by the time I've finished talking to you, my friend, the actor Bob Goodman, is phoning me sometime shortly because he wants to tell me about how he got on. He's got a part in the *League of Extraordinary Gentlemen* movie, and he's just got back from Prague, and he wants to have a chat about how that went. And that's cool. And then, I think Gene Ha's phoning me tonight, as well, about the *Forty-Niners* graphic novel. He probably needs some more pages. So I'll probably be on the phone 'til about 10 o'clock, and then I'm going to be hungry and I'm going to want some food. And then I shall eat the food, that'll be about 11 or something. I'll be up for about another hour, hour and a half after that, just chilling, perhaps reading. Then I'll go to sleep.

I'll get up about half past 8 tomorrow. It'll be about 10 o'clock before I've had breakfast, had a bath, sat around, got myself in the mood to work. And then I shall launch into any one of about four different things, which are all quite urgent at the moment, and which I've got to get done before the end of this week.

There's not really a schedule. I'll get so many phone calls during the day that I can't really plan a work schedule around it. You just have to just kind of fit in the work where you can. I mean, today I had a lengthy phone conversation with a high priestess from

Burkina Faso, who is coming to Northampton to do some ritual magic work on behalf of her tribe, the Dagara. And, since she's coming to Northampton, and since I am kind of the witch doctor of Northampton, somebody told her that she ought to get in touch with me first and that I might be able to help. Which I'm *always* glad to do. My magical life probably takes as much of my time as my comic book life. [General laughter] Perhaps not quite as much, but it certainly takes a chunk of it.

So there's little things. So I just work when I can, you know? And when I can't work, then I eat, or go to sleep, or read a book, or see Melinda. Or sometimes go for a walk in the fresh air. But not very often. [More laughter]

BB: I was going to ask if you needed absolute quiet while working, but that seems like it's a bit of a moot point.

AM: Well, I *do* need absolute quiet, but I don't get it. I live on my own, I work on my own. I don't have music on, or anything else on. I work in absolute silence. All I can hear is the sound of my own thoughts. And then the phone rings, you know?

So I work in silence as much as I can.

BB: Can you work anywhere, or do you basically work at home?

AM: I only work at home, really. This is where I'm comfortable. This is where I've got all the reference that I need. There's not many facts in the known world that I could not uncover by taking six or seven steps from where I'm sitting now. I've got a lot of books around me, I've got a lot of information. And I've got a kettle where I can make my cups of tea. The shop's around the corner, if I run out of tea bags. I've got almost everything I need, so, yeah, I tend to work mostly, or entirely, at home.

BB: My understanding is that you don't care for film very much.

AM: Nope. I've got nothing against it, it's just not my favorite medium. I prefer to read. And if I wasn't reading, I'd probably prefer to listen to a piece of music, or do something else.

I've got a lot of films, and I enjoy a lot of films. But it's not by any means my *favorite* medium. And, in terms of the often-made comparison of writing for films and writing for comics, my position on it is, yes, a comic writer who understands cinematic techniques will be a better comic writer than one who does not understand cinematic techniques. That's obvious. However, if you see comics *only* in terms of cinematic techniques, if you see comics only in terms of cinema, then all it can be is a kind of cinema that doesn't move. They can only ever be is a poor cousin to cinema if *all* they utilize is cinematic techniques. This is why in my work, from *Watchmen* onwards, I've consciously tried to come up with things that comics can do that could not be achieved in any other medium.

There are lots of things that are unique to comics, that comics can do brilliantly, that you can't do in a film. So I think, for the good of the medium, it would be wise to perhaps focus upon those things where comics have an advantage, those things that are unique to comics. The best films are always those that make the use of the unique qualities of cinema. And it stands to reason that the best comic books are probably going to be those that make use of the unique qualities of comics books.

And so, no, film's not a great source of inspiration to me for my work. But I do enjoy a lot of films. Well, I enjoy *some* films. Not a lot. But, generally, I'm not interested in most Hollywood output, you know? And there's generally a better way that I could spend two hours, rather than the sort of movie that every newspaper in the country's telling me to go and watch. I don't have anything against film, but it's not an overwhelming preoccupation for me.

BB: You're not interested in writing for film, then?

AM: Oh, absolutely not. I've been offered. Hollywood has gotten in touch with me many times over the past fifteen years, asking me

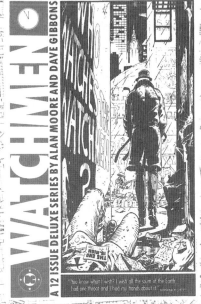

Watchmen™ & ©DC Comics

"This is why in my work, from Watchmen onwards, I've consciously tried to come up with things that comics can do that could not be achieved in any other medium"

to write films, and I would sooner put out my eyes with a rusty coat hanger. The *last* thing I want to do is write films. The only possible reason I could have for writing films is if I wanted the money, and I don't.

I've got complete control in comics. If I put a full stop or a comma down, then it's probably going to end up on the finished page. In movies, I realize that *nobody* has that much control. Every movie is going to be ... You're going to have to do two or three rewrites, which, of course, is going to be anathema to me, and probably they're going to give it to other people to write. The director will be changing around scenes, the actors and actresses will be having their input, depending on how valuable or how big their name is, and, eventually what probably ends up on the screen would have only a coincidental resemblance to whatever I might have written as screenwriter. I mean, there is the famous Hollywood joke about the wannabe starlet who was so *dumb* that she screwed the writer. [General laughter] And I think that's a very *telling* little joke. Probably very accurate.

No, like I say, film's not a medium that is my medium of choice. I don't have a great deal of respect for modern Hollywood, and *that's* probably putting it nicely. And the main thing that I want to do with my work, as I was saying earlier, my main agenda is to get over my thoughts, my world view, things that interest me as *clearly* as possible, in as undiluted a form as possible. I want to get over the things that I think and feel, and I want to get them over to the best of my ability. So control over the work is of absolute paramount importance, and that wouldn't happen if I was working in television, or if I was working in Hollywood. So I know that going in the door, and I don't go in the door. I reject all offers, and generally maintain a kind of haughty, snooty distance from any kind of cinema-related project.

If people want to do adaptations of my books, that's fine. I've got no real interest in the project. I mean, I haven't seen the *From Hell* film. I'm not saying that it's a bad film. I've heard some people say that it's quite a good film. But I just haven't got around to it. Like I say, it's not an abiding preoccupation of mine, the film industry. If they want to adapt my work, if they want to bring out films that may only, again, have a coincidental resemblance to the books, then that's fine. They can give me lots of money and they can go and make a film that has the same title as my book, and maybe some of the same scenes and characters. But at the end of the day, the film and the book, they're two completely separate projects. Whatever the film is like, that makes no difference to what my book was like. If my book wasn't a very good book, and it's a wonderful film, my book is still not going to be a very good book. If my book was a masterpiece, and it's not a very good film, then my book is still going to be a masterpiece. It's kind of irrelevant.

So, "Yes, all cash donations are gratefully received." But beyond that, I don't have a great deal of interest in the film industry.

BB: A few moments ago you mentioned comics' unique qualities. What are some of those qualities that you've had fun exploiting in your work?

AM: Well, *Watchmen* usually provides a good example. With a comic, you have a medium where the reader is very much in control of the material. Somebody reading *Watchmen* can pause and take as long as they want to look one of Dave Gibbons' panels. They can wait until they've spotted every little detail in the background. Or, if they pass on more quickly, they've got the liberty if, in a few pages time, they suddenly find some line of dialogue, some image, that seems perhaps to resonate with something that they saw a couple of pages back, they can flip back a couple of pages and they can say, "Ah, yes, this piece of dialogue *does* relate to that piece of dialogue a couple of pages ago."

They can absorb the book at entirely their own pace. All of the information that you and the artist have crammed into each panel – which in the case of *Watchmen* was considerable, both verbal and visual – they can absorb all that information at entirely their own pace and they can get everything out of the book that you put into it.

Now, with a film, even with a director who customarily uses quite a lot of complexity, like say Terry Gilliam, who at one point was mooted as the director of the *Watchmen* film, Terry Gilliam can get a lot of background detail into his work. But the thing is that the audience is dragged through a film at an unvarying speed of 24 frames per second. Even the most skillful director in the world could *not* put the same layered amount of detail into the background of every shot, and expect his audience to be able to pick it up, to notice it. This gives you possibilities for complexity and richness that a film, which is tied to a strict time frame, can't really offer.

There's also things you can do, like in *Watchmen* when we had the parallel narratives, the boy reading comic book on the street corner. Where, because both the boy reading the comic, and the comic book in which he is appearing, are both comics, you can zoom in from one to the other smoothly. You can have one narrative mirroring, or echoing, or commenting upon the other. This was something I was taking a lot further with *Big Numbers*. I had two or three different layers of fantasy reality that I was playing with in that, although the actual series didn't progress far enough for people to see many of them. But these are things that only comics could do.

Like *Big Numbers*, in that second issue, I think there's a page where I pull off a very show-offy technical trick where I've got a family arguing around a breakfast table. And the whole page is one big picture that's divided up into twelve smaller images. You can read the panels all individually, and if you read them in the regular way they all make perfect sense. But the choreography of the characters enables all the characters to *move* around the page, even though it's one single image, and for their dialogue to keep in the correct order. Now that would be meaningless in cinema. A lot of the aesthetic pleasure of that page is purely to do with the fact that it's comics. It's the fact that there's this really interesting sort of manipulation of time and space that's going on on the page.

Watchmen ™ &©DC Comics

"Somebody reading Watchmen can pause and take as long as they want to look one of Dave Gibbons' panels"

Or think of something like *Promethea* # 12, where the whole issue is a twenty-four page freeze; where you could, if you bought two issues of the book, join all the pages together into one long unbroken panel; where the first page and the last page, furthermore, link up, so that the freeze potentially runs on forever. There's a flip book element worked into it, with little angels go up one side of the page, while little demons go down on the other side of the page. You've got twenty-two Tarot cards which are explaining the entire history of the universe, in counterpoint with scrabble tiles which are rearranging themselves into variants of the word "Promethea" – anagrams which have relevance to the Tarot card *and* the era of world history that are being discussed upon that page. *And* you've got this joke from Aleister Crowley running along the bottom, told by Crowley himself, aging from an infant to a schoolboy to an old man on his deathbed, over twenty-four pages. I mean, there's not another medium in the world that you could do anything like that in. That is except, perhaps, music. It's something like a fugue in music, but, as far as I know, unique to comics.

And this is just scratching the surface. There are *thousands* of wonderful new effects. I mean, if any aspiring comic writers out there, or comic artists, *anybody* looking for new storytelling techniques, they might want to go back and look at some of the great American newspaper strips of the turn of the century. Look at Winsor McCay. Look at Frank King. Those guys were doing stuff that was more experimental and avant-garde than probably most of the stuff you'd have seen in *Raw*, for example. We've done very little to *better* some of those guys in the intervening century, you know? They were delighting in the possibilities of the medium. They were stretching it any way that they could, seeing what new things might be done with comic strips, with combinations of words and pictures, or the *endless*, myriad ways that you can put them together with each other.

I don't think we've scratched the surface. I think that the comic industry – whether commercial concerns will allow it to or not is a different matter – but the comic industry could carry on for centuries and *still* have thousands and thousands of wonderful new approaches and ideas that were actually untouched.

BB: How important *are* business considerations, both generally, and then in your particular case?

AM: Well, I love the comics medium. I pretty much *detest* the comics industry. Give it another 15 months, I'll probably be pulling out of mainstream, commercial comics because ...

Not everybody and every company is a hateful figure. Of course they're not. Most of these are really nice people who are doing their best, you know? But the companies, the business? I don't really have time for it anymore. I'm fed up with this.

All I want to do is to just do the work. But I don't want anybody interfering with it. I don't want anybody telling me that I can't do *this*, or I can't do *that* for some lame, neurotic reason that has *nothing* to do with creativity, and where the person telling me is, frankly, not a person in most instances that I respect creatively – if I respect them upon any level. I'm *probably* a better writer, you know? I should *probably* be allowed to make my own decisions as to how my work comes out I don't seem to be able to find that in mainstream comics, and I am kind of tired of the territory of mainstream comics. I mean, yeah, I can do inventive, new, refreshing things with superheroes from now until the cows come home. But do I *want* to, do I have the spirit for it? No, not really. Not really.

I've *really* enjoyed doing ABC, and I tried to make them as unlike superheroes as it was possible to make, but with the exception of *The League of Extraordinary Gentlemen*, they probably will all wrap up in about fifteen months. Fifteen months, a couple of years. And then, at that point, I shall be focusing upon work which is probably a lot more personal to me, is a lot more uncompromising, where I don't have to have commercial concerns. Where I don't have to *worry* whether anyone's going to like this, buy it, or anything. That doesn't mean that I'm going to be deliberately, willfully difficult. I'm not going to try and do pieces that people won't like, because I'm always very conscious of the fact that I am talking to an audience, and that they don't have to listen to me. *But* I want to be able to do things *completely* as I insist on doing them. And I think that will probably necessitate a move away from the center ground of comics, probably out towards the margins, if not out of comics altogether. I don't know. I mean, I will probably always be doing comics in some form or another, along with all of the other that stuff I do. But that probably won't be mainstream comics for an awful lot longer.

BB: Right, I'd suspect that you'd have a home with Top Shelf and similar-minded publishers.

AM: Absolutely. Top Shelf is a company that I'd *always* be happy to work with. Chris Staros is a gentleman. But, like I say, I'd prefer to move as far away from the center ground as is possible to get, because I *don't* feel comfortable there. I never have.

I mean, when I look back at the twenty-five years I've spent in the industry, there are a *lot* of very pleasant memories. These are all to do with artists, writers, some of the people that I've met and the work that we've done together. There *are* an awful lot of unpleasant memories. These are all to do with companies. So I want the one without the other, you know? I want the *art*, and the collaborations, and the creativity. I want *work* that has creative moments. I want all that. I mean, I want to *die* at the typewriter. I'm in love with all that.

But I am getting to the point where I can not put up with all of this bullshit for another second, you know? Well, I can – for about another fifteen months. [General laughter] And then I'll at least taking a step back, maybe taking some time off. I mean, I know it sounds a bit reckless and wild, but I haven't really had a holiday in twenty years. It'd be nice to take six months off, or something like that, and not do anything. Well, I can barely imagine that, you know? And to just not know what I'm going to do ...

That's what I really want. I want, as with so many middle aged men, at my juncture of life, what I really want is more insecurity and uncertainty. I really don't want security and certainty, and I don't want to know what I'm going to be doing next month, and the month after that, and the month after that. I want to surprise myself, scare myself, whatever. Shake myself up a bit, and *progress*. Yeah, the grazing here is good, you know, and I'm sure I could grow old and fat and contented. Well, I could grow old and fat. [General laughter] But I'd prefer to move on to what's over the next ridge.

BB: Well, with that in mind, combined with the fact that you can basically write your own ticket now, what are some of the things that you'd like to do?

AM: What, for the work to do?

BB: Yeah.

AM: Well, what I might be doing after my retirement, since I can write my ticket, I might write some more song lyrics. More song lyrics, more performance pieces, because I always quite liked some of those songs me and various musicians have done over the years. And me and Tim Perkins, my musical accomplice, we've got an album of songs that we're putting together at the moment. I wouldn't be singing these, I hasten to reassure the public out there. We've got an album of new songs that we're putting together called *Car Ads of the Future*, and I love writing songs.

I mean, writing songs, writing poetry, writing things to be read aloud where they have to have a certain rhythm, a certain cadence, you know? These things are very, very useful if you want to learn how to write comics. I found out, when I used to do performance poetry for the Arts Lab when I was 16, that some poems which look *great* read on a printed page, sound clumsy, and clunky, when read aloud. And I started to realize how important *rhythm* was in almost establishing a hypnotic trance in the mind of the listener or reader, and that's something which I applied to my comics work, sometimes in some of the more flowing passages. I spent ages trimming syllables off words so that I don't suddenly get a clunk in the middle of a sentence. Rhythm is tremendously important.

BB: Is that something you'd suggest writers try to improve their own work?

AM: Yeah, try writing songs. I'm sure that most people out there know a good song when they hear it. They know Elvis Costello from 'N Sync. So try it, try putting lyrics together. You'll see that your *mind* does different *things* when you're writing a song. The creative constraints are different; your mind works differently.

Try writing a novel, without any pictures. You know, that was a very lonely experience. It took me about five years. Probably one of the best things I've ever written. Taught me a lot about writing.

Don't stick with comics writing, not in your reading habits, and not in your writing habits. If you stick within one area, you'll inevitably stagnate. Play the field a little. Write other things. Write films, if that's what you're interested in, write plays. Write poetry, write songs, scribble on walls. Whatever. But every new area that you explore will give you a whole new range of tools and ideas that you can then use to cross fertilize your other work. Comic writing has given me ideas about how to go about writing a novel. Having written a novel, that's given me ideas about how to write comics.

I'd say, try not to limit yourself. There's no reason. Yes, we all went to school, and we had Careers Advice Officers who told us what we would be best suited at in adult life. I think I was told policeman, because I was quite tall, so that obviously marked me down as a sort of defender of law and order. But there's no reason why any of us have to do just one thing. There's no reason why, if you're a writer, you can't be three other things at once. You can be a performer, you can be an artist.

One of the things I shall probably be doing after I reach fifty in sixteen months, is doing a lot more drawing. Because I used to *love* doing that. It wasn't very good, but I have improved. In the years when I've not been doing any drawing at all, I found that I have improved. [General laughter] You know, you'd think that you'd have to practice to improve. But when I kind of, more or less, phased the drawing out, towards the sort of Middle Ages or sometime like that, I wasn't very satisfied with what I could do. When, in the early 90s, I started doing a few color pieces – I did a book dust jacket design for a book [*The Risen* by Peter Whitehead] that came out a few years back, and I did a CD cover [for the Creation Books spoken word CD sampler, *Hexentexts*] – I was very pleased with them. I've come on a bit. And I haven't done much since then, but, yeah, give it another eighteen months, a couple years, I think I might very well be playing around with color crayons and seeing if I can manage it without going over the lines, you know? I don't know what will come of it, maybe nothing. Or maybe just the sort of drawings that are for my private satisfaction only.

But I will enjoy stretching out again, and *playing*. Playing without purpose. Which is basically how I started all of this stuff, when I was giving names and attributes to my crappy plastic toy soldiers at the age of six. All creative stuff, it starts in play.

Try and play. Try and have fun.

I mean, when I'm doing these almanacs for *The League of Extraordinary Gentlemen*, I'm laughing myself sick. I came up with these guides to the imaginary world. I did the one for the Americas a little while ago, and I managed to put an island from Gilbert and Sullivan's *H.M.S. Pinafore* right next to Captain Marsh's island. This is Captain Obed Marsh of Innsmouth, from the Lovecraft stories, and so this island is infested with Lovecraft's subaquatic monsters, nameless terrors from the deep. But I've said, "Look, it's only half a mile from this island where all the *H.M.S. Pinafore* stuff was going on," and, in fact, Captain Corcoran of the Pinafore not only *met* these creatures from the lower depths, but he also taught them to *sing*. And he arranged a sort of special royal command performance for Princess Zara, and, all right, he could only teach them to sing in thick, inhuman, bubbling voices, but he did teach

V For Vendetta ™ & ©DC Comics. Song©V Songs

"Try writing songs. I'm sure that most people out there know a good song when they hear it"

them to sing, and we do have a sample of some of the lyrics of the songs that were specially written for this command performance. So I've got some lyrics that are kind of Gilbert and Sullivan and Lovecraft, and that was fun.

In the African version, I've got the tribe of Babar the elephant living in the same territory where stands the deserted hut, ringed by decomposing heads on poles, where the ivory traders agent Mr. Kurtz enjoyed his reign of terror. [General laughter] And putting Barbar the elephant up against *Heart of Darkness*, you know, perhaps it's just me, but I thought it was funny. "The horror! The horror!"

It's play. It's a kind of silly-assed intellectual play, but it's play. And I'd like to play with the crayons, and perhaps do a bit of sculpture. I don't know. I'm probably not any good at it at all, but I used to like the feel of wet clay on my hands when I was ten. Yeah, I've more or less given up on ever being a ballet dancer, but beyond that, I'm up for anything, really.

BB: It's generally accepted knowledge that you taught Neil Gaiman the basic structure of doing comics, so I was wondering what were some of the things you emphasized to him?

AM: Well, when you say that I taught Neil Gaiman the basic structure of comics, [really, it was] only as much as Steve Moore taught me the basic structure. In that Neil said, "I'm interested in comics. How do you actually write them?" And I think I sat down with Neil and a bit of paper and a biro and said, "Right, at the top of the first page you put, Page One, and then you put Panel One, and then you put your panel description for Panel One on Page One," and I explained how you did that, and what you had to do, and what you had to tell the artist. And then I said, "Then you put your dialogue, and you write that like this, or if you've got a caption, you put CAP. For sound effects you put FX." Sort of all of this stuff – just, basically, easy stuff – and perhaps gave him a couple of pointers as to just very basic stuff. And then Neil did a couple of tryout stories. A kind of a medieval Swamp Thing story, about one of the earlier versions of Swamp Thing, and he did a John Constantine story, and I thought they were both great. And I either sent them to Karen Berger, or suggested that he did, I forget which, but the rest is history.

Yeah, I know that Neil *liked* my work, and probably, his early stories, he was probably influenced a bit by my stuff. But Neil very, very quickly found his own voice and developed into a *remarkable* writer in his own right. I wouldn't want to claim that I'd given Neil a great deal of help. Sort of, I taught him how to lay things out, but, basically, that's all kind of pretty common sense stuff anyway, you know? I might kind of claim that I taught Neil Gaiman everything he knows, if there's some Goth chick that I'm trying to impress, but that's probably lies.

I mean, Neil had always got what it took to be a writer, and he just needed to know the basic mechanics of how to lay a script out. And he was off, really. He *might* have taken a couple licks from my early work, back then when he was starting out. But he soon developed plenty of perfectly adequate licks of his own.

BB: Is there a question you've always wanted to answer, but no one has posed it to you yet?

AM: Will you marry me? [General laughter] That's not a hint by the way, you know? [More laughter]

I don't know, I'm just trying to think ...

Eddie Campbell *did* ask me a question that I've been looking forward to answering for some time in an interview I did with him recently, when he asked me, "How in the world did you go about doing *Promethea* # 12?" And I've been waiting for someone to ask me that so I could crow, and just explain my own brilliance to the world. Just in case they'd missed it. [More laughter]

But, yeah, I went on for pages about what a genius I am, and what an incredibly groundbreaking piece of work this is, so I won't repeat that here. Buy Eddie Campbell's aptly titled *Egomania* and

**"Putting Barbar the elephant up
against Heart of Darkness, you know,
perhaps it's just me, but I thought
it was funny"**

read that one yourself.

But, yeah, I've probably been asked every question that it's possible to ask a person. I don't know. I can't think of too many questions that I haven't answered. "Am I now, or have I ever been, a card-carrying member of the Communist Party?" Well, no, actually.

I can't think of any, Bill. That's probably about it. I can't think of a single question that I haven't been asked in a twenty-five year career that I've always *longed* to be asked. No. I think I'm probably well interrogated by this point.

Snakes and Ladders©2001 Alan Moore and Eddie Campbell

League of Extraordinary Gentlemen ™ & ©2005
Alan Moore & Kevin O'Neill

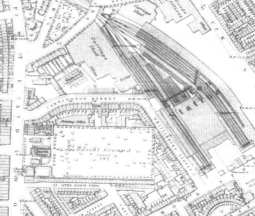

"I can't think of a single question that
I haven't been asked in a twenty-five
year career that I've always longed to
be asked"

Where to Find Alan Moore's Books

An incredibly prolific author, Moore has worked for a wide variety of publishers over the past 25 years, making a complete listing of his works a book-length project in its own right. Also, surprising for a creator this popular, a great deal of his work is also currently out of print or only available in single-issue formats. However, there are a number of very good collections and original graphic novels and adaptations of his work readily available to the interested reader. Below you'll find a short listing of the major publishers offering work by Moore and his many collaborators, along with some short notations of interest.

America's Best Comics, LLC, 7910 Ivanhoe# 438, La Jolla, CA 92037, USA
http://www.DCcomics.com/WildStorm/
ABC, a subsidiary of WildStorm Productions, published the majority of Alan Moore's later commercial comics work, including the entire ABC line of books – including *Promethea, Tom Strong, The Forty-Niners* and *Top Ten* – as well as the first two volumes of the creator-owned *The League of Extraordinary Gentlemen*.

Checker Book Publishing Group, 17 N. Main Street, Suite 31, Centerville, OH 45459
www.CheckerBPG.com
Checker publishes several trades featuring Moore's work for Awesome Entertainment, including the Superman-inspired *Supreme*, an award-winning title.

DC Comics, 1700 Broadway, New York, NY 10019, USA
www.DCcomics.com
DC published much of Moore's seminal work during the 80s and 90s, including *V for Vendetta, Swamp Thing, Watchmen* and various specials, single issues and such. All of Moore's various works, including *The Killing Joke* graphic novel, are being compiled into a single edition, *DC Universe: The Stories of Alan Moore*.

Titan Books, 144 Southwark St, London SE1 OUP, UK
www.2000ADonline.com
Publishers of some of the earliest of Moore's comics work, these folks have also been pretty good about keeping much of these books – including *The Ballad of Halo Jones, The Complete D.R, & Quinch* and *Skizz* – in print and available.

Top Shelf Productions, P. O. Box 1282, Marietta, GA 30061-1282
http://www.topshelfcomix.com/

Publishers of a wide variety of cartoonists, this independent press has fostered and developed strong relationships with a number of creators, including both Eddie Campbell and Alan Moore. So it makes perfect sense that this imprint has published much of Moore's more recent, experimental comics and projects, such as *From Hell, Voice of the Fire* and *The Mirror of Love*. This is also the imprint which will probably be releasing much of his future comics work, including the recently-completed *Lost Girls* and all future *League of Extraordinary Gentlemen* adventures.

Alan Moore is not only an award-winning author of comics, novels, plays and other entertainments, he is also one of the most influential and celebrated creators to have ever worked in the comics industry. He's written any number of highly acclaimed books, including *Miracleman*, *Watchmen*, *V for Vendetta*, *From Hell*, *The League of Extraordinary Gentlemen*, *Promethea* and numerous other graphic novels, as well as done seminal work on the DC

Comics characters Swamp Thing, Superman and Batman. Alan Moore resides quite happily in his native England, amid books, friends and family.

Bill Baker is a veteran entertainment journalist who's been a regular contributor to *Tripwire*, *Cinefantastique/CFQ*, *Comic Book Marketplace*, *International Studio* and other magazines. Bill also hosts an online column called "Baker's Dozen" -- which you'll find at www.WorldFamousComics.com/ bakersdozen – that features short but meaty interviews with comic book and other creators of Pop Culture, and does monthly reviews of graphic novels for the increasingly popular www.Bookslut.com literary webzine under the "gutterslut" moniker. More information on Bill's professional activities can be found at www.BloodintheGutters.com, his home on the web, which he shares with Joel Meadows, the editor/ designer of this book. Bill Baker lives and works in the wilds of the Upper Peninsula of Michigan, USA, for some unknown and quite likely overly complicated reason.